STRICTLY NO CROCS

by Heather Pindar

Illustrated by
Susan Batori

Essex County Council

'Strictly No Crocs'
An original concept by Heather Pindar
© Heather Pindar

Illustrated by Susan Batori

Published by MAVERICK ARTS PUBLISHING LTD
Studio 3A, City Business Centre, 6 Brighton Road,
Horsham, West Sussex, RH13 5BB
© Maverick Arts Publishing Limited May 2017
+44 (0)1403 256941

A CIP catalogue record for this book is available at the British Library.

ISBN 978-1-84886-240-1

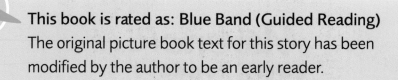

www.maverickbooks.co.uk

Blue

This book is rated as: Blue Band (Guided Reading)
The original picture book text for this story has been
modified by the author to be an early reader.

STRICTLY NO CROCS

by Heather Pindar

Illustrated by Susan Batori

Zebra was having a party.

She asked everyone to come, but ...

...the crocs were not invited.

But the crocs wanted to go to the party.

"We can eat everyone up!" said Cruncher.

"But how will we get in?" said Chomper.

"We can dress up!" said Snapper.

"No one will spot us!"

So the crocs went to the party.

First Cruncher, then Chomper
and then Snapper.

They had a lot of fun!

Cruncher went on the bouncy castle.

Chomper played a game ...

... and he won a bear!

Then everyone sang

'Happy Birthday To You!'

Zebra had a big cake.

Snapper ate too much!

Next it was time to dance.

The crocs sang:

"Na-na na na na na na!"

Everyone had fun
popping balloons.

Bang!

Bang!

Then everyone went outside.

Oooooohhhhhhh!

"I love fireworks!" said Chomper.

Soon the party was over.

Cruncher, Chomper and Snapper said,

"Thank you!" and waved goodbye.

The crocs walked home.

"That was a fab party!" said Chomper.

"Fantastic!" said Cruncher.

"Oh no!" said Snapper,

"We forgot to eat

everyone up!"

"Never mind," said Cruncher.

"It's Giraffe's birthday party next week..."

Quiz

1. What animals are not invited to Zebra's birthday party?
a) Crocodiles
b) Giraffes
c) Lions

2. What does Cruncher bounce on?
a) A bed
b) A bouncy castle
c) A trampoline

3. What does everyone do to the balloons?
a) Pop them
b) Throw them
c) Sit on them

4. Whose party is it next week?
a) Lion's
b) Giraffe's
c) Monkey's

5. What do the Crocs forget to do?
a) Sing 'Happy Birthday'
b) Say 'thank you'
c) Eat everybody up

Turn over for answers

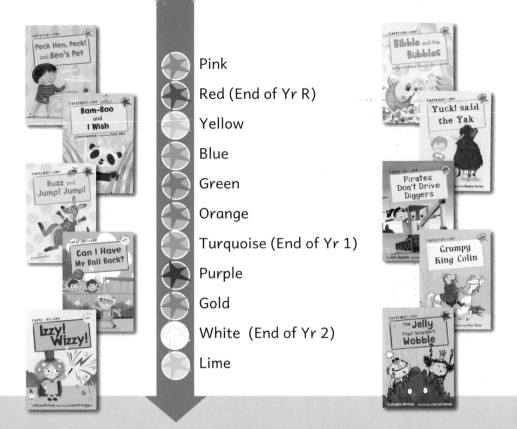

Pink

Red (End of Yr R)

Yellow

Blue

Green

Orange

Turquoise (End of Yr 1)

Purple

Gold

White (End of Yr 2)

Lime

Book Bands for Guided Reading

The Institute of Education book banding system is made up of twelve colours, which reflect the level of reading difficulty. The bands are assigned by taking into account the content, the language style, the layout and phonics.

Children learn at different speeds but the colour chart shows the levels of progression with the national expectation shown in brackets. To learn more visit the IoE website: www.ioe.ac.uk.

Maverick early readers have been adapted from the original picture books so that children can make the essential transition from listener to reader. All of these books have been book banded for guided reading to the industry standard and edited by a leading educational consultant.

Quiz Answers: 1a, 2b, 3a, 4b, 5c